Original title:
The Stag's Path

Copyright © 2024 Swan Charm
All rights reserved.

Author: Olivia Orav
ISBN HARDBACK: 978-9908-1-0229-0
ISBN PAPERBACK: 978-9908-1-0230-6
ISBN EBOOK: 978-9908-1-0231-3

Chronicles of the Emerald Canopy

Beneath the bright green leaves we dance,
Laughter rings as spirits prance.
Sunbeams filter through the trees,
Nature's tunes hum on the breeze.

With every step, the joy ignites,
Colors bloom in dazzling sights.
Festival of life unfurling bright,
Under blue skies and golden light.

Secret paths beckon us to roam,
In the canopy, we find our home.
Songs of birds, sweetly they sing,
In this haven, our hearts take wing.

Cheers echo as shadows sway,
Joyful memories here will stay.
Together we'll chase the setting sun,
In the emerald grove, we are one.

Running with the Wind Through Woods

With the wind, we race and play,
Through the woods, we sprint and sway.
Leaves rustle in a cheerful tune,
Whispers dance beneath the moon.

Every branch a new surprise,
Nature's magic fills the skies.
Footsteps light on forest floor,
Adventure calls, we long for more.

In laughter's echo, time stands still,
Joy cascades down every hill.
Golden rays through branches peer,
In this moment, we hold dear.

Hand in hand, we roam so free,
Windswept dreams and jubilee.
The woods embrace our fleeting flight,
In this revelry, our hearts ignite.

Whispers of the Wilderness Call

The wild calls softly in the night,
Stars above twinkle so bright.
Leaves dance lightly, shadows play,
In the wild, we find our way.

Crickets chirp in a perfect rhyme,
Nature's song, a pulse of time.
Moonlit paths invite our feet,
Where the earth and sky do meet.

Around the fire, tales are spun,
Embers flicker, laughter's fun.
In every whisper, life enthralls,
In this magic, the wilderness calls.

Together we savor every thrill,
Under the stars, our souls are still.
With every heartbeat, the night unfurls,
In this moment, we embrace the world.

Steps Through the Verdant Glade

In the heart of green we'll sway,
With laughter bright to guide our way.
Beneath the boughs where shadows play,
We dance in joy, it's a festive day.

Flowers bloom in colors bold,
Whispers of stories yet untold.
With every step, new wonders unfold,
In the glade, our spirits gold.

Sunlight dapples on our skin,
Nature's chorus beckons us in.
As we twirl, let the games begin,
In the glade, where dreams are kin.

To the tune of a joyful heart,
Every soul here plays a part.
Together we craft an art,
In the glade, where friendships start.

The Dance of Hooves and Leaves

Round the fire, stories soar,
Hooves beat loud on the forest floor.
As laughter rings, and spirits implore,
We dance together, forevermore.

Leaves rustle softly in the breeze,
Joyful whispers flow with ease.
In this moment, time takes a freeze,
We dance as one, hearts at peace.

With every twirl, our worries wane,
Under the moon, we break the chain.
In the rhythm, we're free of pain,
In this dance, love shall remain.

So raise a glass to all we hold,
To bonds unbroken, to stories bold.
In this dance, our lives unfold,
A tapestry of joy retold.

A Wildheart's Solitude

In the stillness of the evening light,
Where nature hums, and stars ignite,
A wildheart finds their pure delight,
In solitude, the world feels right.

With a gentle breeze that kisses skin,
The solitude invites within.
Here is the place where dreams begin,
In quietude, let the heart sing.

As shadows stretch, and dusk descends,
Thoughts take flight like loyal friends.
In this calm, the spirit mends,
A celebration that never ends.

For in the wild, I find my truth,
In every moment, I reclaim my youth.
Embracing silence, like a sleuth,
A wildheart's dance, the essence of proof.

Twilight Among the Trees

As twilight falls, the world aglow,
We gather 'neath where the tall trees grow.
In the fading light, our spirits flow,
With laughter and love, we steal the show.

Fireflies flicker, a merry dance,
Casting soft lights in a starlit trance.
Together we'll enter this blissful chance,
To dance with joy, our hearts askance.

In the embrace of the dusky shade,
We share our tales, never afraid.
In the woods, our worries fade,
In this twilight, friendship is laid.

So let us raise a toast of cheer,
To moments lived, in hearts held dear.
In twilight's glow, the path is clear,
Among the trees, we have no fear.

Whispers and Wildflower Paths

Beneath the sunlit skies so clear,
The laughter dances, bright and near.
With petals swaying, colors blend,
In every corner, joy we send.

As breezes carry scents of sweet,
We share our dreams on twinkling feet.
A tapestry of hearts entwined,
In whispers soft, our hopes aligned.

Traces of the Wayward Spirit

Through meadows lush, we trace our steps,
With every turn, adventure prep.
The echoes of a song so light,
They guide us through the shimmering night.

Beneath the stars, we sing and sway,
Embracing warmth of fleeting day.
The wayward spirit weaves the scene,
In every laugh, we find the dream.

Where the Wild Things Roam

In a forest where the laughter roars,
And playful shadows dance on shores.
The wild things gather, spirits free,
A fervent chant of jubilee.

With open hearts, we share our tales,
Underneath the moonlight veils.
A fest of colors, sights, and sounds,
In nature's arms, true joy abounds.

Eclipsed in the Embrace of Pines

As twilight falls, the lanterns glow,
In gentle whispers, soft winds flow.
The pines surround, their secrets keep,
While joyous hearts begin to leap.

With laughter echoing in the air,
We gather close, adventures share.
Eclipsed in love, our spirits rise,
Within the night, beneath the skies.

The Nature of Solitude

In quiet corners, joy's embrace,
A moment's peace, a gentle place.
Beneath the stars that softly gleam,
Solitude whispers, a joyful dream.

With every sigh, the heart takes flight,
Dancing shadows in the night.
In stillness found, the spirit swells,
In solitude's arms, pure magic dwells.

Paths Woven in Fern

Beneath the boughs, where shadows play,
Fern-clad paths, we laugh and sway.
Each step a song, a melody bright,
Nature's chorus, pure delight.

With laughter ringing, we glide along,
The earth below hums our song.
Woven in green, our dreams take flight,
Together we dance in the soft daylight.

Sounds of Rustling Leaves

Whispers in the breeze, so sweet,
Rustling leaves beneath our feet.
Each crackling sound a story told,
In nature's warmth, we find our gold.

With every rustle, life's refrain,
Echoes softly, joy's domain.
In this symphony, hearts align,
The sounds of leaves, pure and divine.

A Stroll Through Timeless Grove

Under arching trees, we drift and roam,
In this grove, we find our home.
With sunlit rays and shadows cast,
Memories linger, forever vast.

Frolic in the beams that play,
Every moment a bright bouquet.
Time stands still, as we explore,
In timeless grove, we seek for more.

Through thickets and Thorns

In a forest alive with cheer,
The laughter of friends draws near.
Colors burst from every glance,
Nature invites us to dance.

Through thickets and thorns we weave,
Embracing the magic we believe.
Sunlight flickers, a golden spark,
In this joyous, vibrant park.

Whispers of secrets on the breeze,
Songs of the wild make hearts at ease.
Together we share this playful jest,
In this moment, we feel so blessed.

With every step, the joy ignites,
A tapestry of wondrous sights.
Through thickets and thorns we roam,
In nature's embrace, we find our home.

The Call of the Wild Heart

Underneath the open sky,
The echoes of freedom almost sigh.
Adventure calls in a wild refrain,
A dance with the wind, let's break every chain.

With every heartbeat, a story unfolds,
Whispered dreams through the night extolled.
The wild heart throbs with life anew,
In the rhythm of nature, we feel the true.

Fires burn bright, casting flickering light,
Illuminating faces with pure delight.
As laughter rings through the sprawling pines,
In this wild place, the spirit aligns.

Together we bask in the moon's soft glow,
United in joy, we freely flow.
The call of the wild beckons us near,
In this moment, we shed every fear.

A Sojourn Under the Stars

Beneath the vast celestial dome,
We gather together, far from home.
The stars twinkle like diamonds bright,
Guiding our dreams throughout the night.

With blankets spread on soft cool grass,
We share stories as time seems to pass.
The universe dances in harmony,
A perfect night for you and me.

In whispered tones, secrets are told,
The warmth of friendship, more precious than gold.
Galaxies swirl in a cosmic embrace,
In this sojourn, we've found our place.

As dawn approaches, the stars fade away,
Yet in our hearts, they forever stay.
A sojourn under stars etched in our minds,
Memories created, true love binds.

The Dance of Leaves and Light

In the breeze, the leaves swirl and sway,
As sunlight dances, brightening the day.
A joyous ballet upon the trees,
Nature's music carried on the breeze.

Colors burst in a lively embrace,
Each leaf takes its turn, quickening the pace.
Golden rays filter, casting a glow,
In this celebration, our spirits flow.

With each rustle, a story unfolds,
The dance of the leaves, a joy to behold.
Together we spin, lost in delight,
In the symphony of day turning night.

As shadows stretch and twilight descends,
This festive moment, where magic blends.
The dance of leaves and light guides our hearts,
In nature's embrace, where true joy starts.

Tales of the Woodland Majesty

In the glade where shadows play,
The whispers weave of night and day.
Each leaf adorned in amber light,
A dance of ferns, a sweet delight.

The brook hums loud, a joyful tune,
Beneath the watchful, silver moon.
Squirrels leap from branch to nest,
In nature's cradle, all find rest.

Wildflowers bloom in bright array,
As laughter flows in childlike spray.
Joyful spirits roam at will,
In the woodland's heart, we find our thrill.

With every step, the magic grows,
In every rustle, a secret shows.
So gather 'round, let tales unfold,
Of woodland majesty, bright and bold.

Hoofbeats on the Horizon

Thunderous sounds, the earth does shake,
A gathering force, the ground does wake.
Horses gallop, manes catching air,
In festive splendor, beyond compare.

The sun ignites the golden fields,
A tapestry of joy that yields.
Each hoofbeat echoes, strong and clear,
In heartbeats racing, we draw near.

Around the bend, the banners sway,
Colors bright, a grand array.
Laughter spills like sparkling wine,
Together here, our spirits shine.

As twilight falls on the horizon,
The magic holds, we feel the rising.
Hoofbeats fade, yet memories stay,
In festive hearts, they'll never stray.

Embracing the Wild Side

In the forest's vibrant haze,
Adventures beckon through the maze.
With every turn, excitement swells,
As nature's magic casts its spells.

Branches sway with joyous grace,
Nature's heartbeat, a warm embrace.
Among the shadows, laughter rings,
The wild side calls, and freedom sings.

Beneath the stars, we dance and twirl,
With wildflowers, our dreams unfurl.
From mountain peaks to rivers wide,
We'll cherish all, embracing the wild side.

In every moment, pure delight,
Adventure sparkles in the night.
Together we roam, hand in hand,
In this joyous, enchanted land.

Nature's Silent Compass

Within the woods, a compass lies,
In whispered leaves and painted skies.
Through rustling branches, stories flow,
Nature's guide, a gentle glow.

The rivers dance, a winding trail,
With each soft song, the heart sets sail.
In harmony, the world awakes,
With every breath, a joy that breaks.

Bright blossoms bloom, a sign divine,
As sunlight spills like sweetened wine.
A festive spirit fills the air,
With nature's wonders everywhere.

So let us wander, hand in hand,
With nature's compass close at hand.
In every moment, let love steer,
A journey light, together here.

Where the Wild Things Gather

In the meadow where we play,
Joyful laughter fills the day,
Color bursts in every hue,
As the wild things dance anew.

Beneath the sky, so vast and bright,
Fireflies twinkle, soft twilight,
Friendly spirits rise and glide,
As the wild things feel the tide.

Echoing songs from the trees,
Whispers carried by the breeze,
Gathering round, spirits entwined,
Where the magic's not confined.

With hearts alight, we spin and sway,
Chasing stars that come our way,
In the night, our dreams take flight,
Where the wild things gather tight.

Seasons of the Heart in Bloom

Spring awakens, colors gleam,
Petals open, sweetly beam,
Joyful whispers fill the air,
In this season, love's laid bare.

Summer dances in warm light,
Laughter shared beneath the night,
Every heartbeat sings a song,
In this season, we belong.

Autumn's hues in gold and rust,
Leaves descending, memories thrust,
Gathering round, we toast with cheer,
In this season, friends are near.

Winter blankets all in white,
Fires crackle, hearts feel bright,
Holding close, we share delight,
In this season, dreams take flight.

Questing Through Enchanted Shadows

In the woods where secrets grow,
Moonlight dances, soft and low,
Magic whispers through the leaves,
As we gather, hope retrieves.

Shadowy figures flit and glide,
Guiding us where dreams reside,
With each step, the night reveals,
Stories woven, fate conceals.

Stars cascade from skies above,
Kindred spirits, filled with love,
Together we embrace the night,
Questing forth, our souls take flight.

In the dark, our laughter streams,
Chasing ever after dreams,
Through enchanted paths we'll roam,
Hand in hand, we find our home.

The Language of Antlers and Pines

Amid the pines, where shadows play,
Antlers rise in bold display,
Nature speaks in whispers clear,
Echoes of our hearts draw near.

Sunlight dapples forest floor,
Footsteps soft, the wild to explore,
In the rustle, voices blend,
In this realm, we transcend.

Stories etched in bark and stone,
Every step, a world unknown,
Courage found in every glance,
In this space, our spirits dance.

Together, we commune with earth,
Celebrating life and birth,
In the forest, drawn by signs,
Speaking softly, antlers, pines.

Wildflowers Bleeding Joy

In fields where wildflowers bloom and sway,
Colors dance in the golden ray.
Laughter spills on the gentle breeze,
Nature's canvas, a vibrant tease.

Beneath the sun's warm, glowing kiss,
Moments carved in perfect bliss.
Children chase each dream in flight,
A symphony of pure delight.

Petals whisper secrets to the sky,
While butterflies flutter, oh so spry.
Joy spills forth from every stem,
In the wild, we find our gem.

So raise a glass to the bright array,
In wildflower fields, we'll forever play.

Antlered Dreams at Dawn

The dawn breaks with a glimmering glow,
Antlered shadows in the soft meadow.
Whispers of dreams hang in the air,
As nature wakes with fragrant flair.

Sunbeams kiss the dew on grass,
A magical hour, moments pass.
Elk roam freely, proud and grand,
In the peace of this quiet land.

Birdsong weaves through the waking trees,
An invitation carried by the breeze.
Hearts feel light, spirits soar,
In the morning's embrace, we crave more.

With antlers raised to the glowing sun,
The day is bright, let the feast begun!

Journeying Beyond the Ordinary

Step beyond the mundane path we tread,
Where whispers of adventure are widely spread.
Through valleys lush and mountains high,
We chase the dreams that light the sky.

With friends beside and hearts aglow,
We dance through fields where wild winds blow.
Every mile, a story unfolds,
With laughter shared, a memory holds.

Through vibrant markets and starlit nights,
In every shadow, wonder ignites.
Tasting life in colors bright,
As joy ignites our endless flight.

So grab your pack, let's wander wide,
In the journey, our hearts abide.

The Hidden Heartbeat of the Grove

Within the grove, where whispers play,
A heartbeat thrums in a mystical way.
Tall trees sway with secrets to tell,
Their leaves rustle like a gentle bell.

Sunlight filters through the boughs,
Painting shadows, life arouses.
In the cool embrace of green and shade,
Friendship blooms, never to fade.

Little critters join in the cheer,
As the hidden heartbeat draws us near.
Laughter echoes in nature's choir,
Stoking the flames of our heart's desire.

So let us gather, beneath the sky,
In the grove, where spirits fly.

Echoes of a Woodland Journey

Leaves whisper tales in the wind's embrace,
Sunlight dapples the forest's face,
Joyful laughter rings through the trees,
In this woodland, hearts find ease.

Mushrooms sprout like little stars,
Nature's wonder, near and far,
Breezes carry a playful tune,
In the shade of the afternoon.

Squirrels dance in the golden light,
Life unfolds, a pure delight,
Bark and branch in harmony sway,
As we wander, come what may.

With every step, the magic grows,
Through vibrant paths where adventure flows,
This woodland journey, pure and bright,
Celebrates a heart's delight.

A Dance of Shadows and Light

Moonbeams flicker on the forest floor,
Whispers of night invite us to explore,
Fireflies twinkle like stars on earth,
In this moment, find your worth.

Branches sway in a gentle kiss,
Nature's ballroom, a scene of bliss,
Silhouettes waltz with grace untold,
Stories of magic, brave and bold.

Cool night air carries dreams anew,
In shadows, friendships bloom and grew,
Hand in hand, we lose our fear,
As laughter mingles with the cheer.

In this dance, where hearts ignite,
We celebrate the joy of night,
Under the stars, together we sway,
In this festive, lively play.

Feathers on the Wind

Softly gliding 'neath a bright blue sky,
Birds take flight, their spirits high,
Each feather tells a story bold,
Of adventures waiting to unfold.

A chorus rings from the leafy trees,
Nature's symphony carried on the breeze,
Wings embrace the sunlit air,
A festive dance, free from care.

Colors splash as they soar and dive,
In the wild, we feel alive,
Every flutter, a spark of cheer,
Revealing joy that draws us near.

With each flap, the world feels bright,
Boundless dreams take fearless flight,
Under the sky, where hearts blend,
In this moment, joy transcends.

Graceful Tracks in the Snow

Footprints trace a story in the white,
Winter's canvas, a pure delight,
With every step, laughter rings,
As nature weaves her festive strings.

Hats and gloves, all bundled tight,
Warm hearts shining, oh so bright,
Snowflakes dance, a joyful show,
Creating magic down below.

Sleds are racing, joy takes flight,
In this season, spirits ignite,
Chasing dreams through the winter chill,
With every laughter, time stands still.

In twilight hours, a glow appears,
As we gather, sharing cheers,
Graceful tracks in the snow proclaim,
Our hearts entwined in winter's game.

Antlers Against the Sky

Beneath the stars, the antlers stand,
A silhouette, so proud and grand.
With laughter ringing through the night,
We dance beneath the soft moonlight.

The forest whispers tales of old,
Of joy and dreams, you can be bold.
A fire crackles, stories weave,
In every glance, we dare believe.

The echoes of our laughter sing,
As lights of joy, our hearts they bring.
We celebrate the magic here,
In every smile, no room for fear.

With antlers raised, we greet the morn,
In festal clothes, our spirits worn.
Together in this vibrant glow,
A bond so strong, forever flow.

Wild Dreams and Forest Schemes

Wild dreams dance in the moonlit air,
With forest schemes, a world so rare.
We gather close, where shadows meld,
In nature's heart, our spirits held.

Beneath the trees, the echoes play,
As golden leaves swirl in ballet.
With laughter bright, the night ignites,
In every step, our joy takes flight.

Adventures sparked by stars above,
In forest realms, we pledge our love.
Through whispers sweet and breezes mild,
We find the wonder of the wild.

With arms outstretched, we claim the night,
In wildness wrapped, where dreams take flight.
Together we will laugh and scheme,
In endless joy, we find our dream.

On the Edge of the Woods

On the edge where shadows play,
We gather bright as dawn's first ray.
With hearts aglow, we share the cheer,
In every laugh, our love is clear.

The woods invite with gentle grace,
Where every step finds its own place.
In rustling leaves and whispers sweet,
We share our hopes, our lives complete.

Bright lanterns float on evening's breath,
In unity, we hold the depth.
With stories spun and bonds we weave,
On this edge, we dare believe.

Together now, our spirits soar,
From whispered dreams, we seek for more.
In vibrant nights, our joy alive,
On the edge, together we thrive.

A Journey of Grace and Grit

With every step, we greet the dawn,
A journey paved; our fears are gone.
Through laughter loud and moments bright,
We find our strength, our hearts ignite.

In paths untraveled, dreams take flight,
With every turn, we chase the light.
Through valleys deep and mountains tall,
In unity, we conquer all.

The rhythm of our laughter swells,
While nature shares her secret spells.
In every challenge, grace we find,
In grit and harmony combined.

A tapestry of hearts and minds,
In each small act, the joy unwinds.
Together we will face the day,
In grace and grit, we lead the way.

Timid Hearts in the Wilderness

In twilight's glow, we gather near,
With whispers soft, we share our cheer.
The air is sweet, with laughter bright,
In timid hearts, the flames ignite.

A dance of shadows, joy takes flight,
Beneath the stars, the world feels right.
With every step, we chase our dreams,
In unity, we hear love's themes.

Around the fire, stories unfold,
Each tale a treasure, each laugh pure gold.
We welcome night with open hearts,
As festive spirit in us starts.

Together we stand, hand in hand,
This wilderness, our joyful land.
With every twinkle from above,
We celebrate our bond and love.

Echoes from the Eldritch Forest

In shadows deep where whispers play,
The forest sings at close of day.
With silver beams that softly glance,
The trees invite us, join the dance.

Beneath the boughs, the secrets hum,
In every leaf, a song, a drum.
The echoes call, our spirits rise,
In this wild place, there's no disguise.

With hearts ablaze, we twirl and spin,
Each step we take, we feel within.
The magic flows, we're lost in time,
Together weaving tales, sublime.

Laughter twines with nature's breath,
Embracing life, defying death.
In eldritch woods, our joy takes form,
A festive night, a sacred warm.

Pathways of the Celestial Wanderer

With every step the stars align,
A cosmic path, a drink of wine.
We stroll beneath a velvet sky,
Where wishes soar and dreams can fly.

The moonlight dances on our skin,
Inviting all our souls to spin.
Through boundless night, we roam so free,
As celestial voyagers, you and me.

In laughter's echo, we find our way,
Guided by starlight's soft array.
In every heartbeat, rhythms sway,
As festive dreams paint night and day.

A tapestry of light and hope,
Together, love, we learn to cope.
On pathways bright, our spirits glimmer,
As joys abound, our hearts grow thinner.

Resounding Silence in Leafy Halls

In leafy halls, where secrets dwell,
A silken hush, yet all is well.
With nature's voice, we hear the sound,
Of joy and peace all around.

The rustling leaves, a calming tune,
In harmony with stars and moon.
Together here, our laughter spills,
In silence bold, we share our thrills.

With every glance, a spark ignites,
Beneath the trees, our hearts take flight.
In quiet moments, we find delight,
As festive vibes create the night.

The gentle breeze, our whispered cheer,
Wraps us in warmth while drawing near.
In leafy halls, our spirits sing,
A tranquil joy that love can bring.

The Footprints of Ancient Dreams

In fields where laughter dances high,
The echoes of the past float by.
With each step, we rediscover,
The joy that binds us, sister, brother.

Around the fire, stories bloom,
Illuminated in the evening's gloom.
Unity in hearts, a vibrant thread,
Festive spirits, where dreams are led.

Candles flicker in the night,
Casting shadows, a warm delight.
We trace the paths that time forgot,
Every moment cherished, never sought.

The night is young, the stars ignite,
We dance beneath the moonlit light.
With every heartbeat, love flows free,
In ancient dreams, we find our glee.

The Luminescent Trail of the Olden Grove

In the grove where whispers sing,
Joy and laughter take their wing.
Beneath the branches, shadows play,
A tapestry of night and day.

Lanterns gleam with golden light,
Guiding us through the calming night.
Nature wraps us in her embrace,
As we whirl in a festive space.

The leaves are rustling in delight,
A symphony of soft insight.
Together we weave, unite, and share,
In olden grooves, our hearts laid bare.

Songs erupt like blooms in spring,
Every note a joyous wing.
With laughter ringing through the trees,
We ride the waves of gentle breeze.

Beneath the Horned Moon

Under the watch of the horned moon,
We gather, swaying to a tune.
Firelight flickers in joyful cheer,
As laughter dances, near and dear.

Stars are bursting, a festive show,
Echoes of dreams, they softly flow.
With friends around, the night feels bright,
In the moon's embrace, hearts take flight.

The cool breeze carries tales of old,
Memories woven, bright and bold.
In this circle, warmth ignites,
Filling our spirits with pure delights.

So let us sing till dawn awakes,
The bonds we forge, the joy it makes.
Under the horned moon, we are free,
In unity found, we simply be.

Nature's Timeless Passage

In the garden where wonders grow,
Nature whispers secrets low.
Sunshine weaves through branches high,
A glorious dance, a festive sky.

Petals fall like confetti bright,
Celebrating the day's sweet light.
With every bloom, a tale unfolds,
Adventures shared, futures bold.

The rivers hum a merry tune,
While crickets chirp beneath the moon.
Hand in hand, we roam and play,
In nature's arms, we glide away.

With laughter ringing like silver bells,
In timeless passage, magic dwells.
So come, my friend, let's take a chance,
In nature's fest, let's laugh and dance.

Echoing Beats of the Hidden Realm

In the woods where shadows play,
The drums of joy begin to sway,
Laughter mingles with the night,
As stars above begin to light.

Colors dance in flick'ring flames,
While whispers call each other's names,
A tapestry of joy unfolds,
Echoing tales of the bold.

Footsteps tapping on the ground,
New friendships cherished, newly found,
In every heartbeat, every cheer,
The hidden realm draws us near.

So let the music fill the air,
In this moment, free from care,
Together we will paint the sky,
With every laugh, our spirits fly.

The Silent Pursuit of Freedom

In meadows green where petals bloom,
Hope whispers soft in twilight's gloom,
Every heart beats with delight,
As dreams take flight in fading light.

Breezes carry tales of grace,
As we move with vibrant pace,
Chasing shadows, lost in cheer,
Celebrating all we hold dear.

The moonlight wraps us in its glow,
Guiding us where dreams can grow,
So let's dance beneath the stars,
In the night, we'll forget our scars.

With every step, our spirits rise,
In the silence, hear our sighs,
For freedom calls in joyful tones,
In hearts united, we find homes.

Veils Between the Bark and Sky

Beneath the trees where shadows weave,
Magic stirs, we dare believe,
With every rustle, nature sings,
Celebrations of simple things.

Veils of mist in morning's light,
Dance with joy, with pure delight,
Leaves flutter like notes in a tune,
As laughter wakes the sleeping moon.

Branches arch in warm embrace,
Welcoming life, a sacred space,
In the whispers, secrets soar,
Nature's kingdom forevermore.

So gather close, in peace we share,
A union formed without a care,
In the realm where hearts entwine,
Together we, in joy, align.

Starlit Routes of the Heart

Across the paths where starlight gleams,
Our wanderings are woven dreams,
With every step, the night ignites,
A tapestry of pure delights.

Laughter echoes through the skies,
Underneath the moon's soft sighs,
Hand in hand, we'll chase the night,
Creating memories of sheer delight.

The universe spins in our cheer,
As we find adventure near,
In every twinkle, every glance,
Our hearts unite in joyous dance.

So take a breath, let sorrows part,
And travel forth with open heart,
For on this journey, love's the art,
We'll walk the starlit routes of heart.

Moonlit Meadow Wanderings

Beneath the moon's soft glow, we dance,
In meadows wide, where dreams enhance.
The stars above, like lanterns bright,
Guide our steps through the joyful night.

In whispers sweet, the flowers sway,
As silver beams light up our play.
Laughter rings through the balmy air,
Each moment cherished, beyond compare.

A gentle breeze brings tales anew,
Of wandering souls, and love that's true.
With every step, our spirits soar,
In this sweet haven, forevermore.

Echoes of the Antlered Heart

In the forest deep, where shadows blend,
The antlered heart calls, a festive friend.
With echoes bright, it leads the way,
Through rustling leaves, where dancers sway.

A gathering swells by a flickering fire,
The heartbeat of nature, lifting us higher.
Soft melodies drift on the crisp night air,
As we join in joy, free from every care.

With every laugh, new stories unfold,
Of ancient woods and spirits bold.
The night is alive, a vibrant art,
In the echoing rhythm of the antlered heart.

The Wilderness Beckons

The call of the wild sings through the trees,
With rustling leaves, carried on the breeze.
A symphony bright, of chirps and cheers,
The wilderness beckons, silencing fears.

Under canopies draped in moonlit sheen,
Every shadow dances, enticing and keen.
With every footfall, adventure awaits,
As magic whispers through nature's gates.

Songs of the night weave tales of delight,
While fireflies twinkle, painting the night.
With open hearts, we embrace the spree,
In the wilderness' arms, wild and free.

Strides Through the Undergrowth

With each stride forward, the world unfolds,
In vibrant greens and stories untold.
The undergrowth teems with life and cheer,
A festive spirit that draws us near.

Sunlight dapples through leaves up high,
As laughter dances with the butterfly.
We wander on paths, side by side,
Each step a journey, a joyful ride.

Petals flutter like confetti bright,
As the day unfolds in warm sunlight.
With nature's embrace, we feel alive,
In every stride, our spirits thrive.

Wandering Where Wind Whispers

In the glade where shadows dance,
Laughter twirls on breezy chance.
Colors twinkle, spirits soar,
Echoes of joy forever more.

Whispers weave through ancient trees,
Bringing tales upon the breeze.
Footsteps light and hearts so free,
In this realm of jubilee.

Sparkling lights like stars descend,
Nature's song, a joyful blend.
Warm embraces, smiles abound,
In the magic, love is found.

Wandering through this festive air,
With each moment, love to share.
The wind's soft sigh, a sweet surprise,
In this haven where joy lies.

In the Realm of Fern and Moss

Where the ferns in green array,
Frolic in the light of day.
Mossy carpets, soft and bright,
Invite us into sheer delight.

Every corner, life abounds,
Chirping birds and joyous sounds.
Sunlight flutters through the leaves,
Whispers of what the heart believes.

Together we'll weave tales anew,
In this world, both fresh and true.
Dancing shadows, laughter's call,
In this realm, we'll have it all.

Celebration in every breath,
A festive pulse, defying death.
Here amidst the green we find,
Cherished moments for heart and mind.

A Journey Through the Glade

Step by step, we roam and play,
In the glimmering light of day.
Flowers nod in colors bright,
Nature's canvas, sheer delight.

Songs of laughter fill the air,
Adventure waits for those who dare.
Every turn, a spark, a glow,
In this journey, hearts will flow.

Here, the trees like towers rise,
Stretching hands toward the skies.
Together, let us venture forth,
In the glade, we find our worth.

Moments captured, memories made,
In this enchanting, fleeting glade.
A festive sprinkle on the soul,
As we dance, we feel whole.

The Enchanted Woodland Quest

In twilight's glow, we start our quest,
Through wooded paths, we seek the best.
Candles lit by fireflies bright,
Guide us gently through the night.

Every rustle, every cheer,
Leads us onward, drawing near.
With each laugh that breaks the gloom,
We find magic, we find bloom.

Following whispers, soft and sweet,
In this quest, our hearts will meet.
Joy adorns both day and night,
In this woodland, pure delight.

Together, hand in hand we stroll,
As laughter fills and warms the soul.
In the quest, our spirits rise,
Underneath the starry skies.

An Oath to the Earth Beneath

Underneath the golden sun,
We gather with hearts full of cheer,
Whispers of nature's sweet song,
Remind us that love is near.

Hands joined in this sacred pact,
With laughter that dances and swirls,
We pledge to protect and revive,
This treasure of greens and twirls.

In fields where the blossoms bloom bright,
And streams flow with life's gentle grace,
Together we celebrate the earth,
In every warm, loving embrace.

So let's raise our voices in joy,
For the wonders the world shares free,
An oath to the lands we hold dear,
Forever in harmony be.

Solitary Reflections Beneath the Boughs

Beneath the grand, whispering trees,
A moment of silence unfolds,
Here, thoughts drift like autumn leaves,
In a dance of stories retold.

The sunlight dapples the soft ground,
As shadows play hide and seek,
Each rustle a gentle reminder,
That peace in solitude speaks.

In this timeless embrace of calm,
The heart finds a rhythm, a beat,
With a chorus of nature around,
Life's melodies weave so sweet.

So linger a while in this space,
Let your spirit rejuvenate,
For beneath the boughs overhead,
A treasure of stillness awaits.

Mysterious Glimmers of a Hidden Path

In the gloaming where shadows play,
Whispers of mystery beckon close,
With each step, a spark draws near,
Enticing the heart to wander, engrossed.

Glimmers of starlight shine through leaves,
As moonbeams dance on the dew,
A secret route only revealed,
To those who are open and true.

The air hums with tales of the night,
As owls call and crickets sing,
Every corner a hint of the past,
Where wanderers' dreams take wing.

So follow the thread of these whispers,
Embrace every crooked turn,
For the path holds treasures unseen,
And adventures waiting to burn.

Tracing Stories on the Forest Floor

A blanket of leaves whispers soft,
Beneath our feet, life's tale unfolds,
Each crinkle and crunch holds a secret,
Stories of love and courage bold.

Footprints of ages long gone,
Trace through the moss, rich and deep,
Each mark a reminder of journeys,
In slumber or dreams that we keep.

The dance of shadows and light,
Creates a canvas both old and new,
With the laughter of springs long past,
Painting the earth with every hue.

So let us tread softly and lightly,
And honor the paths that we roam,
For on this vibrant forest floor,
We find traces of our true home.

The Call of Dappled Light

In the meadow where colors blend,
Joyful laughter seems to send.
Sunbeams dance on the leafy green,
A festive spirit can be seen.

Bubbles float in the gentle air,
Children's giggles everywhere.
Candles flicker in twilight's glow,
The warmth of friendship begins to flow.

Banners sway in soft summer breeze,
Nature's orchestra fills with ease.
Voices rise like birds in flight,
Together we bask in the light.

As shadows stretch and day will fade,
Promises linger, memories made.
Heartfelt dreams weave through the night,
Celebration under stars so bright.

Serpentine Callings in the Woods

Twisting paths through vibrant trees,
Nature whispers in the breeze.
Rustling leaves like laughter shared,
In this haven, nothing is spared.

Creatures scurry, join the dance,
In the wild, come take a chance.
Glowing fireflies light the dark,
Each flicker ignites a spark.

Mushrooms bloom in radiant hues,
Underneath the sky so blue.
Happy songs fill the balmy air,
As we wander without a care.

Branches sway to a hidden beat,
Enchanting all who dare to meet.
In this world, the joys unfold,
Serpentine tales in colors bold.

Footfalls on Forgotten Routes

Once lost paths now brightly lit,
With every step, new joys we hit.
Old stones sing of times long past,
Echoes of laughter start to last.

Paths lined with flowers, wild and free,
Invite us to ponder, to see.
With every footfall, memories bloom,
Reviving the heart, dispelling gloom.

Sunset paints the evening sky,
Beneath its glow, we stand nearby.
Stories linger in the gentle breeze,
Whispers of dreams among the trees.

Together we walk on this sacred ground,
In every heartbeat, a love profound.
As the stars twinkle, our spirits rise,
On forgotten routes, we're truly wise.

Harbingers of the Forest Silence

In the stillness, magic lies,
Where shadows dance and silence flies.
Whispers in the trees align,
Nature's lullabies softly entwine.

Crickets chirp a soothing song,
Lulling night where we belong.
Moonlight bathes the world in grace,
Every creature finds its place.

Stars twinkle like festive cheer,
Their shimmering glow draws us near.
In moments hushed, hearts unite,
Together we bask in sacred night.

As dawn approaches, colors burst,
With every sunrise comes the thirst.
For celebration, for delight,
In forest silence, endless light.

Shadows and Light Under the Canopy

In the grove where laughter rings,
Sunlight weaves through fluttering leaves.
Colors dance on the soft earth,
Whispers of joy in the heart it cleaves.

Butterflies pirouette in the air,
Blooming flowers paint the scene bright.
Children chase shadows, giggles alive,
In this haven of warmth and light.

Beneath the branches, stories unfold,
Echoes of love in festival's sway.
Candles flicker as night draws near,
The stars join our dance in a celestial play.

Together we gather, hand in hand,
Bonds strengthened in laughter and cheer.
Under the canopy, hearts intertwine,
In the tapestry of memories, dear.

Traces of Serenity in Nature

Gentle breezes hum a soft tune,
Flowers nodding in the warm sun's gaze.
Rivers giggle, reflecting the sky,
Nature's jewels set our hearts ablaze.

Birds trill in harmony, pure and bright,
Dance through the branches, flit about.
Every note lifts spirits high,
In this serene world, there's no doubt.

Sunsets spill gold across the lake,
Glimmers sparkle like stars set free.
Peace wraps around, a tender skin,
In the cradle of nature, we are filled with glee.

As moonlight softens the day's glow,
Together we sigh, tranquility's muse.
In each moment, a blessing found,
In nature's embrace, we choose to lose.

Nature's Embrace through Time

In the woods where stories weave,
Ancient trees whisper their lore.
Roots entangle in a warm embrace,
Time stands still at nature's door.

Seasons bloom with life anew,
Colors shifting like the tides.
Each leaf fluttering sings a tale,
In this haven where joy abides.

Mountains rise, kissing the sky,
Rays of sunshine break the day.
Streams murmur secrets, sweet and pure,
As children frolic in wild array.

In harmony, we share this space,
Moments captured like fleeting dreams.
Nature's canvas, forever alive,
In her embrace, our spirits beam.

Where Hope Meets the Horizon

At dawn, the sky begins to glow,
Hints of magic in the waking light.
Birdsong breaks the early hush,
A promise of joy, horizon bright.

Waves crash gently on the shore,
Each drop sparkling like dreams reborn.
Footprints lead to distant places,
In this dance of life, hope is sworn.

Fields of gold sway in the breeze,
Creating a symphony with every turn.
Bright blooms shout of life's delight,
In the garden where passions burn.

As daylight folds into a starry night,
We gather close, hearts intertwined.
Together we share our whispered hopes,
Where the horizon draws all kinds.

Whispers of Ancient Woods

In the glade where shadows play,
Leaves dance lightly on the sway.
Sunbeams sip the dewdrop's glow,
Ancient whispers softly flow.

Birdsong trills a cheerful sound,
Nature's breath is all around.
Footfalls on the forest floor,
Echo tales of days of yore.

Mossy boughs and fragrant pine,
Adventure calls through ages fine.
With every step, a laugh or cheer,
Festive spirits draw quite near.

In this realm of verdant green,
Joy and magic can be seen.
Heartbeats match the wood's delight,
Whispers weave through day and night.

The Quiet Majesty of the Marvelous

Mountains rise with regal grace,
The world wrapped in a sweet embrace.
Colors bloom, a vibrant sight,
Underneath the stars so bright.

Rivers weave like silver thread,
Past the field where dreams are bred.
Nature's canvas, vast and bold,
Stories of the earth unfold.

Gentle breezes carry song,
In this realm, we all belong.
Each moment, laughter fills the air,
Magic lingers everywhere.

So raise a toast to wondrous play,
Find the joy in every day.
For in nature's glowing crown,
Quiet majesty abounds.

Navigating Through Nature's Labyrinth

In a maze of towering trees,
Whispers float upon the breeze.
Paths entwine like tales we weave,
Hiding treasures to believe.

Colors splash where wildflowers bloom,
Sunshine banishes the gloom.
Birds in chorus take their flight,
Guiding hearts through day and night.

Every turn reveals delight,
Nature's wonders, pure and bright.
Join the dance of leaf and vine,
Festive spirits intertwine.

As we wander ever free,
Laughing by each blossom's spree,
In this labyrinth, we'll reside,
With nature's magic as our guide.

Harmony in the Wild

Dancing shadows, twinkling lights,
Nature's symphony ignites.
Whispers of the ancient trees,
Carried gently on the breeze.

Streams serenade the glade,
In their ripples, joy is laid.
Vibrant blooms in colors bright,
Celebrate the pure delight.

Together, creatures share their song,
In this wild, we all belong.
Heartbeats sync with nature's choir,
Lifting spirits ever higher.

With every step, the laughter flows,
In harmony, the wild bestows.
A festive cheer, so wild and free,
Embraced by all we see.

Heartbeats in the Glade

In the glade where laughter sings,
Joyful hearts encounter spring.
Colors dance beneath the trees,
Whispers float upon the breeze.

Children run with cheerful glee,
Nature's child, wild and free.
Every step, a beat in time,
Lost in love, a heart's sweet rhyme.

Bubbles rise with giggles bright,
Sunbeams twirl in pure delight.
Beneath the sky, so vast and blue,
Every moment feels brand new.

As evening sets the world aglow,
Fireflies put on their show.
Together, dancing all around,
In the glade, pure joy is found.

Spangled Moments of Twilight

Twilight casts its velvet spell,
Whispers of a secret tell.
Stars awaken, softly gleam,
Life unfolds, a waking dream.

Shadows stretch and colors blend,
A painted sky as day must end.
Laughter flows like gentle streams,
Every heart ignited, beams.

Gathered friends with stories old,
Magic moments to be bold.
With every spark, a memory made,
Underneath the twilight's shade.

Songs abound, the night is young,
In harmony, our voices sung.
Together here, as night began,
Spangled moments, hand in hand.

Guardians of the Silent Wood

In silent woods where shadows play,
Guardians watch before the day.
Trees stand tall with wisdom deep,
Secrets held for those who seek.

Crickets sing their evening tune,
Underneath a silver moon.
Branches sway with gentle grace,
Nature's quiet, sacred space.

With every step, the forest breathes,
Life abounds among the leaves.
Hushed whispers echo through the air,
Each heartbeat feels the magic there.

Together in this ancient land,
Hold my heart, and take my hand.
In the stillness, dreams take flight,
Guardians of the gentle night.

Twilight's Breath Upon the Trail

Twilight's breath along the trail,
Scent of pine in evening's veil.
Footsteps soft on earth's embrace,
Every turn a new-found grace.

Colors fade as stars ignite,
Glimmers dance in soft twilight.
Every heartbeat whispers low,
Into the night we gently flow.

Moonlight drapes a silken thread,
Leading dreams where wishes spread.
In this hour, our spirits soar,
Together, we will seek for more.

Time may pause, within this place,
Magic lingers, soft as lace.
Onward we wander, hearts aglow,
Twilight's breath, our guiding flow.

The Trail Beneath the Emerald Canopy.

Through leaves of green, the sunlight plays,
A dance of shadows on forest ways.
Laughter echoes, joyous and bright,
As we wander beneath the light.

Butterflies flutter in bright arrays,
Their colors spark joy on this festive day.
With every step, the wonders unfold,
Stories of nature, timeless and bold.

Wildflowers bloom, a vibrant sight,
Painting the ground with colors so tight.
A gentle breeze whispers through the trees,
Carrying laughter like a sweet tease.

With friends beside, we share the thrill,
Adventures abound on this wooded hill.
The trail beneath the emerald dome,
Calls all to wander, to laugh, and to roam.

Whispers of the Forest Trail

In the forest where secrets lie,
Whispers of laughter, the trees sigh.
Breezes hum a cheerful tune,
Under the warm and glowing moon.

Children's giggles weave through the air,
Nature's melody, a joy to share.
Every step, a note in the song,
As we journey where we belong.

The trail ahead, with stories to tell,
Of sun-kissed blooms and the gentle swell.
With hearts so light and spirits free,
We embrace the magic, just you and me.

As twilight falls, the stars ignite,
The forest sparkles, a wondrous sight.
With every heartbeat, the night unfolds,
In whispers of joy, our adventure holds.

Secrets Beneath the Canopy

Every leaf hides a secret smile,
Nature's wonders, each petite mile.
Under the branches, tales come alive,
In this haven, our spirits thrive.

Groves of laughter surround our trail,
Memories linger, like a soothing veil.
With every footfall, joy intertwines,
Among the trees, our bliss resigns.

Sunlight dapples, casting its glow,
Upon the path where wildflowers grow.
In this bliss, our hearts plant seeds,
Of laughter, love, and simple deeds.

With dusk approaching, the air grows sweet,
As creatures stir beneath our feet.
Together we share, beneath the sky,
The secrets of the forest as time stands by.

Antlers in the Twilight

In twilight's hush, the shadows dance,
Where antlers rise, there's a fleeting chance.
Majestic forms in the fading light,
Whispering secrets of the night.

With every rustle, life draws near,
The forest alive, we pause to cheer.
A gathering here, beneath the swell,
Of starlit skies where stories dwell.

Festive tales of nature's play,
As day surrenders to night's ballet.
Gentle creatures arise from their hide,
In this serene space, we feel the tide.

Together we breathe in the night's embrace,
With laughter echoing through this place.
Twilight cradles the forest dear,
As dreams take flight on the wings of cheer.

Whispers of the Forest Trail

Amidst the leaves, a laughter flows,
A gentle breeze, where sunlight glows.
Colors dance in vibrant cheer,
Nature sings, the joy is near.

Twinkling lights in branches sway,
Echoes of a bright array.
Each footstep whispers tales of play,
In the heart of the woodland fray.

Squirrels darting, quick and spry,
While birds above in chorus fly.
A symphony of woods does ring,
As every creature joins to sing.

Come gather 'round, let spirits rise,
Underneath the vast blue skies.
In this forest, hearts entwine,
Where every moment's pure divine.

Echoes in Antlered Shadows

In twilight's glow, the whispers call,
Shadows stretch, both long and tall.
Antlers gleam with starlit grace,
A timeless song in this enchanted space.

The moonlight weaves a silver thread,
Where woodland paths and dreams are bred.
A dance of echoes, soft and bright,
Beneath the canopy of night.

Fawns frolic in the soft, cool grass,
As time in nature seems to pass.
The rustling leaves seem to conspire,
In this realm of wild desire.

As laughter lingers in the air,
Joyful spirits, free from care.
In antlered shadows, life abounds,
A magical pulse in soft, sweet sounds.

Journey of the Winding Thicket

Winding paths of green and gold,
Adventures rich, waiting to unfold.
Each step taken, a story begins,
Where laughter echoes, joy always wins.

Berries bright and flowers bold,
Whispers of tales yet untold.
The sun peeks through the leafy dome,
In this thicket, we find our home.

A trail adorned with nature's charms,
Each creature calls, with open arms.
Footprints mark where dreams have danced,
In every twist, new hopes are chanced.

So gather your friends, take a stroll,
Let the vibrant thicket console.
In every bend, adventure's near,
A journey of joy, a festive sphere.

Beneath the Canopy's Gaze

Beneath the canopy, hearts unite,
In emerald shadows, pure delight.
The rustling branches softly sway,
As nature gathers for a play.

Glimmers of sunlight burst through leaves,
Painting paths where magic weaves.
Gentle whispers float on high,
As laughter mingles with the sky.

Every creature plays its part,
In this festival of the heart.
From chirping birds to buzzing bees,
A chorus carried on the breeze.

So come and dance beneath the trees,
In joyous rhythm, feel the ease.
In this haven, where spirits blaze,
We celebrate beneath the gaze.

Reflections in the Silent Wood

In the forest where whispers play,
Leaves dance brightly in the sway.
Sunlight filters through the trees,
A world alive with vibrant ease.

Birds sing sweetly, joy unfolds,
Nature's magic, a tale retold.
Each rustling branch, a happy song,
A moment cherished, where we belong.

Laughter echoes through the glade,
Children's smiles, a masquerade.
Gathered close, we share delight,
As day gives way to falling night.

Stars emerge, a twinkling crown,
The forest wears its twilight gown.
With friends beside, our spirits soar,
In silent woods, we cherish more.

Call of the Untamed Way

Wanderers tread the wildest path,
The heart ignited, sparking wrath.
Laughter rings through valleys wide,
As bonfires blaze and hearts confide.

Beyond the hills, the spirit flies,
Underneath the vast, open skies.
Adventures wait with eager grace,
In every corner, magic's embrace.

Echoes sing of times not past,
Where dreams are bold and shadows cast.
United in the thrill we find,
As nature calls, we leave behind.

With arms outstretched, we greet the day,
In the rhythm of the untamed way.
A festive heart, we twirl and sway,
Unleashed in bliss, forever play.

Secrets of the Moonlit Clearing

In the hush of night, we gather round,
Moonlight spills o'er the silver ground.
Magic threads weave through the air,
Unveiling secrets, hidden and rare.

The nightingale croons a soothing tune,
While lanterns glow beneath the moon.
Fingers pointed at the sky,
We share our dreams, let hopes fly high.

Whispers float on the gentle breeze,
As hearts entwine with elegant ease.
The clearing dances with life anew,
Inviting laughter, a spark for two.

With each sweet story shared that night,
In treasured moments, hearts take flight.
Under the stars, we claim our part,
In moonlit shades, we find pure heart.

A Track Through Time's Embrace

A winding path through ancient trees,
Where echoes of laughter ride the breeze.
Each step a tale, a memory's trace,
In nature's arms, we find our place.

The sun dips low, painting skies bright,
As day transforms to velvet night.
With friends beside, we laugh and sing,
In timeless moments, joy we bring.

Footprints linger along the way,
Stories etched in night and day.
Celebration blooms in every heart,
As time unfolds its treasured art.

In this embrace, we live, we play,
Grateful for each festive day.
Clinging to joy like leaves to trees,
In the tapestry of memories.

Beneath the Canopy's Embrace

Under a sky woven tight,
The twinkling stars come into sight.
Laughter dances on the breeze,
Whispers of secrets in the trees.

Friends gather close, joy ablaze,
In the soft glow of twilight's haze.
Unity found in nature's song,
Where hearts and spirits all belong.

Colors burst in a vibrant spree,
With every sound, we feel so free.
Beneath the leaves, our dreams take flight,
In this festive, enchanted night.

Melodies weave through branches high,
Under the laughter, the moon will sigh.
Each moment cherished, forever stays,
Here in the heart of our joyful ways.

Footprints in the Dappled Light

Through the woods where sunshine spills,
Footprints tell of laughter and thrills.
Every corner, a story to share,
In the dappled light, we breathe the air.

Children's giggles, echoes so sweet,
Nature's rhythm, a festive beat.
With every step, the joy expands,
Together we wander, hand in hands.

The forest winks with vibrant cheer,
Every rustling leaves brings us near.
Moments captured, forever bright,
In this dance of shadows and light.

Together we sing, our spirits soar,
Making memories we all adore.
With every shadow, and every sight,
We leave our footprints in the light.

Tales from the Verdant Verge

At the edge where the green meets the blue,
Tales of wonder await me and you.
Every leaf holds a story told,
In the whispers of young and old.

Colors bright as the sun's embrace,
In this magical, sacred space.
Nature's pageantry, a joyful sight,
We celebrate life in the soft twilight.

Fairy laughter in the breeze so sweet,
For every heart, a rhythmic beat.
Gathered together, hand in hand,
In this festive land, forever we stand.

Under the arch of branches high,
Where the sky and earth seem to tie.
With tales woven in every breath,
We share our dreams, defying death.

A Serenade to the Forest Spirits

In the heart of the woodland glow,
Where the softest breezes flow.
We gather to sing our sweet refrain,
A serenade for the spirits' gain.

Flashes of color in playful flight,
With every song, we embrace the night.
Dancing shadows, a harmonious play,
As the stars above begin to sway.

Upon the stage of rustling leaves,
The forest whispers, and the heart believes.
Together we weave this lively art,
Filling the world with joy from the heart.

Laughter weaves through the emerald air,
In this sanctuary, free of care.
As spirits gather 'neath the moonlit beams,
We find our magic, fulfilling dreams.

Chronicles of Silence and Sound

In the hush of laughter, bells ring clear,
Ghosts of joy dance, drawing us near.
Voices weave stories, a vibrant thread,
Silent whispers blend where dreams are spread.

Fires flicker brightly, casting shadows wide,
Footsteps echo softly, a festive guide.
In the symphony of lives intertwined,
Every note, a memory, beautifully defined.

Carols mingle sweetly, hearts open wide,
Under starlit heavens, spirits abide.
Connection ignites like the warmest flame,
In this joyous union, we all feel the same.

Time stands still as the moments unfurl,
Wrapped in a tapestry, life starts to swirl.
Chronicles written in laughter and cheer,
A celebration of silence, the sound of the year.

Wild Roads of the Heart

With each step we take, the wild winds blow,
Mapping our journey where wildflowers grow.
Paths over mountains, through valleys we roam,
In this dance of freedom, we find our home.

The rhythm of footsteps, a drums beating bright,
Guided by moonlight and stars shining white.
Our spirits unbound like the birds in the sky,
Chasing the sunsets, where colors comply.

Adventurers gather, with laughter so loud,
Sharing our stories, a jubilant crowd.
In the embrace of nature, we feel so alive,
Among wild roads of the heart, we thrive.

Each trail we uncover, a song yet unsung,
Voices resounding, forever we're young.
Traveling together, no need for depart,
This is our journey, the wild of the heart.

The Spirit of the Untraveled Way

In the hush of the forest, whispers beckon,
Adventures await where no footsteps reckon.
Among the tall trees, secrets softly sway,
The spirit of wonder, the untraveled way.

Sunlight dances through leaves, a gleaming delight,
Guiding our senses, igniting the night.
With laughter and stories, we gather around,
Celebrating paths that are yet to be found.

Echoes of dreams rush like rivers below,
Where hearts beat as one, with rhythm and flow.
In the spirit of laughter, we open our minds,
Finding ourselves in the beauty that binds.

Together we journey, with spirits so free,
Embracing the unknown, just you and me.
In the circle of friendship, bright and gay,
We honor the spirit of the untraveled way.

In Pursuit of the Unseen Path

Beyond the horizon, where dreams often play,
In pursuit of the unseen, we dance on the sway.
With hearts wide open, we venture and roam,
Exploring the magic, discovering home.

The air filled with laughter, the joy intertwined,
In the embrace of the moment, true peace we find.
With each twist and turn, our spirits take flight,
Chasing the shadows and basking in light.

Gathering memories, like stars in the night,
In pursuit of the unseen, we'll chase what feels right.
With every shared smile, connections grow tight,
In this tapestry woven, life feels so bright.

Together, we wander through whispers and chance,
In pursuit of adventure, lost in our dance.
With hearts as our compass, we'll forge our own way,
In the celebration of life, we'll forever stay.

www.ingramcontent.com/pod-product-compliance
Ingram Content Group UK Ltd.
Pitfield, Milton Keynes, MK11 3LW, UK
UKHW022125231224
452783UK00011B/408